COOKING WITH WEED

CAUJUAN AKIM MAYO

Copyright © 2015 Caujuan Mayo

UPROCK PUBLICATIONS

All rights reserved.

ISBN:0692518657

ISBN-13: 978-0692518656

www.uprockpublications.com

Getting Started

» Before we get started cooking with weed, we have to make some weed cooking oil and butter which will be used for all recipes.

FOR COOKING & BAKING - CANNABUTTER

Cannabutter

For Cooking & Baking

2-4 hours PREP TIME

» This easy recipe will get you started making Cannabutter, which can be used for most of your cooking and baking needs. Keep in mind the stronger your herb, the stronger your butter. I recommend a 1/2 ounce to an ounce depending on your tolerance for this recipe.

🛒 SHOPPING LIST

- 1 cup butter (2 sticks)
- 1/2 ounce cannabis (shake)
- 2 cups water
- Metal strainer or Chees cloth
- Medium pan
- Glass bowl or plastic container

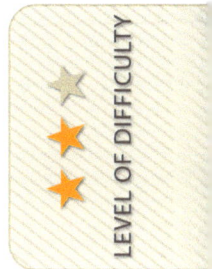

LEVEL OF DIFFICULTY ⭐⭐⭐

🍲 DIRECTIONS

1. Add water and butter to pan over medium heat. Make sure there is enough water to create a layer between butter and the bottom of the pan. Use extra water if necessary.

2. Add cannabis to pan and mix thoroughly

3. Simmer on low heat for 2-3 hours. Stir occasionally to prevent scorching. If mixture starts to boil, reduce heat.

4. Allow pan to cool before straining into bowl or container.

5. Place mixture in fridge overnight. The butter will seperate from the water and rise to the top.

6. Once butter has risen to top, remove from fridge. Peel off the chunks with a fork or knife and place in seperate container.

Canna Oil

For Cooking & Baking

» Any affordable virgin olive oil works great for this recipe. You can cook with canna oil in any recipe that calls for oil.

🛒 SHOPPING LIST

- 3 cups olive oil or canola oil
- 1 ounce cannabis buds, finely ground, or 2 ounces trimmed leaf, dried and ground

45 minutes PREP TIME

🍲 DIRECTIONS

1. In a heavy saucepan (or a double boiler), slowly heat oil on low heat for a few minutes. You should begin to smell the oil's aroma.

2. Add a little bit of cannabis to the oil and then stir until it is fully coated with oil. Keep adding more cannabis until the entire amount of cannabis is mixed into the oil.

3. Simmer on low heat for 45 minutes, stirring occasionally.

4. Remove the mixture from the heat and allow it to cool before straining.

5. Press the cannabis against a metal strainer with the back of a spoon to wring all the oil out of it. Throw the leftover cannabis in the trash.

6. The oil is best stored in an airtight container in the refrigerator for up to 2 months.

LEVEL OF DIFFICULTY ★ ★ ★

Weed French Toast

BREAKFAST FOOD

10-15 minutes PREP TIME

» This is a very easy no fail recipe for french toast. It won't take long to make at all, and it's quite good.

LEVEL OF DIFFICULTY

🛒 SHOPPING LIST

- Whipped Cream
- Bread
- Cannabis butter
- 4 Eggs
- Syrup
- Chocolate sauce
- 2/3 Cup of Milk
- Cinnamon
- 1 tsp Vanilla extract

🍳 DIRECTIONS

1. Heat up normal butter in a pan (don't use your cannabis butter… If you add too much heat, the THC will become less strong and you won't get as HIGH).

2. Separately, combine the vanilla extract, the eggs, the cinnamon and the milk in a bowl and mix them together.

3. Now take your bread and put it in the mixture, then place it in your normally buttered pan.

4. Cook the toast until it is golden brown, flipping it when necessary. When the toast is done, you spread the cannabis butter all over the toast.

5. Now add whipped cream, chocolate sauce, can even add a possible fruit. Enjoy!

Cannabis Blueberry Biscuits

BREAKFAST FOOD

» Enjoy these tasty one of a kind blueberry biscuits. Perfect in the morning for breakfast or a mid day snack.

SHOPPING LIST

- 2 – 2 1/2 cups self-rising flour
- 2 1/2 cups fresh blueberries
- 1/2 cup powdered sugar
- 3/4 – 1 cups milk
- 1/4 cup sugar
- 1/2 cup cannabutter
- 3 tablespoons of milk/water mix

DIRECTIONS

1. Heat oven to 350 degrees.

2. Add the flour and sugar in to a bowl and mix them together well. Then, add your cannabis butter to the mix. Don't melt the butter prior to adding it. If the butter is rock hard, you can let it sit to soften up a bit but you have to keep it in a solid form.

3. beat the butter in to the flour and sugar mix until most of the chunks have disappeared. Then add your blueberries!

4. Next, add the milk. Mix the milk in well until the substance has turned in to a dough. Make sure that it's not too soupy. You can add more flour if necessary or more milk if it's too thick. But it should be more like dough, not like muffin mix. Lay out some flour on a flat surface and begin to knead the dough.

5. Saute the chopped onion in butter in a large frying pan until tender, and let it cool.

6. When the dough has been thoroughly kneaded, get a cookie sheet and grease it well. You don't want the dough to stick to the pan when you're trying to eat it. Take pieces off of the dough and mold them in to small round shapes, 1/2" thick and 2" wide. You must remember to watch them carefully while they cook, as they might end up getting too big. Cook them for 10-20 minutes but keep a close eye on them.

LEVEL OF DIFFICULTY

Cannabis Coffee Cake

» You'll love this easy to bake Cannabis-infused Coffee Cake with your morning coffee. What a great way to start your day.

SHOPPING LIST

45 minutes PREP TIME

- 2 and ¼ cups flour
- 1 package active yeast
- 6 tablespoons vegetable shortening
- 2/3 cup milk
- 6 tablespoons sugar
- 1/4 teaspoon salt
- 1 egg
- 1/2 cup sliced almonds
- 1 and ½ tablespoons cannabis butter (melted)

DIRECTIONS

1. In a medium mixing bowl add I cup flour and the package of active yeast. Set it aside.

2. Take a medium saucepan and add the milk, vegetable shortening and 4 tablespoons of sugar.

3. Heat the pan and stir occasionally. Once the vegetable shortening has softened. Remove the mixture from the heat and add the contents to the yeast and flour mixture.

4. Now add an egg and with an electric mixture best ingredients for one minute. Remove mixture from the sides of the bowl by scraping it and continue to beat the mixture for another 3 to 5 minutes.

5. Slowly stir in the rest of the flour and form pliant dough.

6. Use the nonstick cooking spray to grease the baking pan. If you do not have a cooking spray grease it conventionally.

7. Place the cake mixture into the baking pan. Sprinkle the top of the dough with sliced almonds and the remaining sugar. Cover it with a clean and damp dish cloth and keep aside for one hour to allow the dough to rise. Will normally take an hour or so.

8. Preheat oven to 375°F. remove the dish cloth and drizzle the risen dough with melted cannabis butter. Bake for 17 to 20 minutes. Allow to cool. Slice, eat and feel AMAZING!

LEVEL OF DIFFICULTY

Rasta Pasta

ITALIAN FOOD

>> Have spaghetti one night and fettuccine later! This delicious pasta recipie can be used for many different italian dishes. Swap out noodles for your favorite pasta and enjoy!

10-15 minutes PREP TIME

🛒 SHOPPING LIST

- 12 oz Fettuccine
- 3/4 cup CannaButter
- 1 cup green peas
- 1 can button mushroom pieces

- 1 can portobello mushroom pieces
- 1 cup roasted red peppers
- 2 Clove chopped garlic
- 2 cups light cream (or 1/2&1/2)

- 1 cup grated Parmesan cheese
- 1/2 tsp pepper
- Salt to taste

🍲 DIRECTIONS

1. Cook Fettuccine (drain, cover set aside)

2. In a large skillet melt cannabutter over medium heat

3. Add garlic saute 1-2 minutes

4. Stir in 3/4 cup cream

5. Stir constantly over medium heat 2-3 minutes

6. Add fettuccine, red peppers and mushrooms to skillet

7. Stir in remaining cream, cheese, pepper and salt

LEVEL OF DIFFICULTY

Pot Pasta Sauce

» This is a great sauce you can use for pasta. Even better when used as a pizza marinara.

🛒 SHOPPING LIST

- 1 can tomato paste (6 oz)
- 1 cup water
- 1/2 cup Canna Oil
- 2 cloves garlic, minced
- 1/2 tablespoon dried basil
- 1/2 tablespoon dried oregano
- 1/2 teaspoon pepper
- 1/2 teaspoon salt
- 1/2 tablespoon dried rosemary

🍲 DIRECTIONS

1. Mix all ingredients in small saucepan and stir well.

2. Bring mixture to a light boil.

3. Turn heat to low and simmer for 30 minutes. Stir occasionally.

4. Remove pan from heat, let cool.

5. Transfer cooled sauce to mason jar and cover.

6. Chill sauce in refrigerator for 2 hours before serving for best flavour. Shake occasionally.

LEVEL OF DIFFICULTY ★★☆

30-120 minutes PREP TIME

Pizza

ITALIAN FOOD

40 minutes PREP TIME

>> Making this delicious homemade pizza is as easy as 1, 2, 3! Why order delivery service when you can make it yourself.

🛒 SHOPPING LIST

- 1 cup Cannabis Pizza Sauce   - ½ cup mozzarella cheese, shredded   - ½ cup Romano cheese, shredded
- 1 Prepared Pizza Dough (Store-bought)

🍲 DIRECTIONS

1. Prepare pizza dough by following directions on package label. Preheat oven accordingly. (Usually 400 degrees.)

2. Spread Cannabis Pizza Sauce evenly on top of dough.

3. Sprinkle cheese evenly on top of sauce. Add extra toppings as desired.

4. Bake in oven for 18 to 25 minutes (or as dictated on dough packaging), until cheese is

    golden brown. Note: Some store-bought pizza dough can be baked directly on the oven rack, others may require a

    baking sheet or pizza stone. Be sure to read your label.

LEVEL OF DIFFICULTY

Chicken w/Cannabis Black Bean Sauce

15-25 minutes PREP TIME

DINNER MEAL

>> This is a very easy and savory dish to prepare that your taste buds are gonna love and thank you for after.

🛒 **SHOPPING LIST**

- 1/4 cup cannabis olive oil
- 2 tbsp cornstarch
- 1 tbsp black beans
- 2 chicken breasts, boneless skinless
- 1 tbsp soy sauce
- 2 tbsp chopped garlic
- 1 tbsp chopped red chili
- 1 chopped green onion
- 1/2 tsp sugar
- 1/4 tsp salt
- 1 tbsp cooking wine

LEVEL OF DIFFICULTY ★★★

📋 **DIRECTIONS**

1. Cut chicken into one inch cubes, coat in cornstarch.

2. Heat 1 tbsp oil in a saucepan and stir-fry the chicken until cooked through.

3. To make the sauce, in a separate pan add the cannabis olive oil, black beans, garlic, green onion, wine, salt, sugar and soy sauce and heat on low for about ten minutes.

4. Toss the cooked chicken into the sauce and serve with the chopped red chili on top.

Baked Bud Patatoes

» This triple baked patato is the perfect way to get baked!

SHOPPING LIST

- 4 large potatoes
- 4 tablespoons light brown sugar
- 1/4 cup sour cream
- 1/4 cup CannaButter
- salt and pepper to taste
- cheese (optional)

120 minutes
PREP TIME

DIRECTIONS

1. Preheat oven to 375 degrees. Place potatoes on a baking sheet and bake until tender (about an hour).

   until evenly combined. Mix in 1 cup of flour. Add additional flour if needed to form a soft dough.

2. Remove from oven and allow the potatoes to cool. Cut off the top of each potato, lengthwise.

3. Scoop out the insides while making sure the skin still holds its shape.

4. Mix the scooped potato flesh, sour cream, Cannabutter, salt and pepper together. Mix until very smooth.

5. Stuff the potato mixture back into the potato skins. Bake in oven for 10 minutes or until tops begin to brown.

6. Add toppings as desired. Eat and enjoy!

LEVEL OF DIFFICULTY

Ganja Sweet Patatoes

DINNER MEAL

90 minutes PREP TIME

» There's nothing sweeter than these ganja sweet patatoes. The perfect and healthy side dish to any meal, especially dinner!

🛒 SHOPPING LIST

- 1 teaspoon vanilla extract
- 1 egg
- 2 tablespoons fresh lemon juice
- 1/4 teaspoon ground ginger
- 2 pounds sweet potatoes, peeled, cooked and mashed

- 1/4 teaspoon ground cinnamon
- 1/4 teaspoon ground nutmeg
- 1/3 cup CannaButter, softened
- 1/4 cup evaporated low-fat milk
- 1/2 cup firmly packed light brown sugar

🍲 DIRECTIONS

1. Preheat oven to 350 degrees. Grease a casserole dish (9"x13") in preparation.

2. Combine all ingredients in a large mixing bowl. With a mixer, beat until smooth.

3. Transfer potato mix to casserole dish. Bake uncovered for 45 minutes or until top begins to brown.

LEVEL OF DIFFICULTY

Tasty Tilapia

» As improbable as it might sound, this combination is utterly fantastic, both savoury and refreshing at the same time.

40 minutes PREP TIME

🛒 SHOPPING LIST

- 4 tilapia fillets
- 3 tablespoons fresh lemon
- 1 clove garlic
- 1 teaspoon dried parsley
- pepper to taste
- 2 tablespoons Cannabutter, melted

🍲 DIRECTIONS

1. Preheat the oven to 375°F (190°C). Spray a baking dish with non-stick cooking spray.

2. Rinse tilapia fillets under cool water, and pat dry with paper towels.

3. Place filets in baking dish. Pour lemon juice over fillets. Sprinkle with garlic, parsley, and pepper.

4. Bake in preheated oven until the fish is white and flakes when pulled apart with a fork, about 30 minutes.

5. Briefly remove the fillets, drizzle cannabutter on them, and stick them in the oven for another 2 minutes.

6 Remove from the oven and serve warm!

LEVEL OF DIFFICULTY

Rice & Bean Soup

DINNER MEAL

» Emmm, great for those cold and winter days!

SHOPPING LIST

- 8 tablespoons THC olive oil
- 2 16-ounce cans black beans
- ½ cup chopped yellow onions
- 2 green onions, diced
- 4 cloves garlic, finely chopped
- 1 tablespoon chili powder
- 1 teaspoon dried sage
- 1 bay leaf
- 3 cups cooked long-grain white rice
- Salt
- 1 tablespoon fresh lime juice
- Sour cream
- Sriracha hot sauce

DIRECTIONS

LEVEL OF DIFFICULTY

1. Get a cooking pot with a lid and combine 6 cups of water, yellow onions, beans (drained), green onions, chili powder, garlic, cumin, sage and bay leaf. Put the lid back on the pot and bring to a boil. Reduce the heat and simmer for 10 minutes.

2. Add the long-grain rice, cover the pot ¾ way, and cook for 10 more minutes. Be sure to stir the pot for time to time and add salt and lime juice before serving.

3. Serve the dish in small bowls, adding a tablespoon of THC olive oil to each bowl with a bit of hot sauce and sour cream.

Cream Of Cannabis Soup

» As improbable as it might sound, this combination is utterly fantastic, both savoury and refreshing at the same time.

25 minutes PREP TIME

SHOPPING LIST

- 3 cups vegetable stock
- 4 tablespoons cannabutter
- 1 cup broccoli florets, chopped
- ¼ cup yellow onion, diced
- 1 cup celery, chopped
- 1 tablespoon flour
- 2 cups heavy creamer

DIRECTIONS

1. Bring vegetable stock to a boil in a large pot over high heat. Add broccoli and cook for 5 minutes.

2. Melt the butter in a medium saucepan over medium heat, then sauté the onion and celery for 3 minutes.

3. Stir in the flour, making a thick mixture.

4. Add this mixture to the pot and turn the heat down to a light simmer. Add cream and simmer for 5 minutes.

   The soup should become thick. Serve right away and enjoy! (cheese optional)

Cannabis Hummus

DIPS & SPREADS

10 minutes PREP TIME

» This is my favorite recipe for hummus. With its smooth taste, texture and euphoric effect. You're gonna love how this dip makes you feel.

🛒 SHOPPING LIST

- 1/4 cup tahini
- 2 garlic cloves
- 1/4 cup lemon juice, freshly squeezed
- 1/4 cup Canna Oil
- 1/2 cup ground cumin
- 15 ounce can of chickpeas, drained and rinsed
- 2 tablespoons water
- Salt and pepper to taste

🍲 DIRECTIONS

1. Combine lemon juice and tahini in blender. Blend for 30 seconds.

2. Add chickpeas, garlic, Canna Oil, cumin and water. Blend for 1 minute until smooth. Add more water if needed to reach desired consistency.

3. Pour hummus in serving bowl or store in refrigerator for later.

LEVEL OF DIFFICULTY

Ganja Guacamole

DIPS & SPREADS

15 minutes PREP TIME

» This is a classic guacamole recipe, made with ripe avocados, cilantro and lime. The jalapeno gives this guacamole a great kick, while the Ganja gives your body a nice high.

🛒 SHOPPING LIST

- 2 cloves garlic, minced
- ½ cup THC oil
- 1 jalapeno pepper

- Juice from 2 limes
- 1 teaspoon salt
- ½ cup firmly packed cilantro, chopped

- 1 cucumber, peeled skin and seeds removed, diced
- ½ cup chopped green onions, white and green parts
- 4 avocados, peeled skin and pits removed, one pit reserved

🥣 DIRECTIONS

1. Combine all the ingredients in a blender or food processor.

2. Blend until the mixture is nice and smooth.

3. Add the blended guacamole to a serving bowl.

   Refrigerate any leftovers in an airtight container. Best used within 1 day.

LEVEL OF DIFFICULTY

Cana-Nellini Bean Dip

DIPS & SPREADS

» Cannellini beans are sometimes labeled white kidney beans, in case you're having trouble finding them. Also, dried beans can be substituted for the canned beans if you prefer. Use 1 1/2 cups cooked beans for each 15-ounce can of beans called for.

20 minutes PREP TIME

SHOPPING LIST

- 3 tablespoons finely chopped fresh chives
- 1/2 cup olive canna-oil
- 1/2 teaspoon freshly ground black pepper
- 1 teaspoon kosher salt

- 1 medium garlic clove, coarsely chopped
- 1 tablespoon Worcestershire sauce
- 1 tablespoon white wine vinegar
- 2 (15-ounce) cans cannellini beans, drained and rinsed

DIRECTIONS

1. Place beans, vinegar, Worcestershire, garlic, salt, and pepper in the bowl of a food processor. With the motor running, add canna-oil in a thin stream until completely incorporated and mixture is smooth, about 1 minute.
2. Add chives and pulse 5 times to evenly incorporate. Serve with wheat crackers, radishes, or cucumber and carrot sticks.

LEVEL OF DIFFICULTY ★ ★ ★

Italian Weed Dressing

DIPS & SPREADS

» If you're looking for a way to spice up your salad, then this recipe will definitely do the trick!

5 minutes PREP TIME

SHOPPING LIST

- 1/2 cup Canna Oil
- 1/3 cup red wine vinegar
- 1/4 cup romano cheese, grated

- 3/4 tablespoon sugar
- 1 teaspoon dried basil
- 1 teaspoon dried oregano

- 1/4 teaspoon garlic powder
- 1/4 teaspoon red pepper flakes
- 1 teaspoon black pepper, freshly ground

DIRECTIONS

1. Combine all ingredients in a mason jar.

2. Close lid tightly and shake vigorously for 15 seconds.

3. Serve immediately or store in refrigerator for up to 2 weeks. Always shake before serving.

Weed Fudge

SNACKS & DESSERTS

» Have fun and try adding your favorite nuts, marshmallows, or candy to make a new fudge every time.

120 minutes PREP TIME

LEVEL OF DIFFICULTY

🛒 SHOPPING LIST

- ¼ Cup Canna butter
- 3 Cups Semisweet Chocolate Chips
- 1 (14 oz) CanSweetened Condensed Milk

🍲 DIRECTIONS

1. In a saucepan and on Medium heat, stir everything together until Chocolate and Cannabutter have melted and all have combined

2. Transfer Fudge mixture into a greased 8×8 inch baking dish and refrigerate for 2 Hours

SNACKS & DESSERTS - WEED COOKIES

Weed Cookies

» It can take a lot of practice to get the taste and texture of these cookies perfect, But when you do, oh is it so worth it!

10-15 minutes PREP TIME

🛒 SHOPPING LIST

- 2 cups of all-purpose flour
- 1 teaspoon of baking soda
- 1 teaspoon of salt

- 1 cup of Canna butter
- 1/2 cup of white sugar
- 1/2 cup of brown sugar

- 1 teaspoon of vanilla extract
- 2 eggs and 2 cups of chocolate chips
- 1 cup of finely chopped nuts (optional), replace with more chocolate chips if you don't like nuts

🍲 DIRECTIONS

1. Place your Cannabis butter into a bowl.

2. Grab another small bowl and combine the flour, baking soda, and salt. In the bowl that has your cannabis butter, add the white sugar, and vanilla and mix it.

3. Now add one egg, beat until it is fully mixed, add the other egg and repeat. Continue to mix as you slowly add the flour mixture from the small bowl.

4. When fully mixed stir in the chocolate chips and nut mixture. If your dough mix Is too dry and hard then add a small amount of water and mix until slightly sticky.

5. Separate your dough mixture into five or six smaller balls of dough, and place them on a very lightly greased baking sheet. Preheat your oven to 375 degrees.

6. Place the baking tray into the oven and let it bake for around 10-12 minutes, or until they look cooked! They should be a golden brown color.

7. Let you cookies fully cool, preferably on a wire rack. They are now ready to eat!

LEVEL OF DIFFICULTY
★ ★ ★

Ganja Cheesecake

» This is a nice twist on an original cheesecake recipe that's simple and best of all, irresistibly scrumptious!

6 hours PREP TIME

🛒 SHOPPING LIST

- 1/2 cup finely ground graham crackers
- 5 tablespoons Canna Butter, melted
- 1/3 cup sugar

- 1/8 teaspoon salt
- 4 large eggs
- 1 cup plus 1 tablespoon sugar

- 1 pound sour cream
- 2 teaspoon vanilla extract
- 3 8-ounce packages cream cheese, softened

🍲 DIRECTIONS

1. Invert the bottom of a 9X9-inch springform pan, "lock" the pan's side with the latch and butter the pan with Canna Butter. Stir together all crust ingredients in a bowl. Press onto the bottom and 1 inch up on the sides of the buttered pan. Fill immediately.

2. For the filling, put rack in middle of oven and preheat oven to 350 degrees.

3. Beat cream cheese in a large bowl with mixer on medium speed until fluffy.

4. Reduce speed to low and add eggs, one at a time, mixing well after each addition.

5. Add 1 cup sugar and 1 tablespoon of vanilla and mix until well combined, scraping down sides of bowl with spatula.

6. Put springform pan with crust on a baking sheet with sides to catch any drips.

7. Pour the filling into the crust Bake until cake is set 3 inches from edges, but center is still slightly wobbly, about 45 minutes. Cool in pan on a rack for 5 minutes. Leave oven on.

8. For the topping, stir together the sour cream, the remaining 1 tablespoon of sugar and remaining 1 teaspoon of vanilla in a medium bowl.

9. Drop spoonfuls of topping around edges of cake and then spread evenly over top.

10. Bake cake for 10 minutes more.

11. Run knife around edges of the cake to loosen it, then allow to cool completely in the pan on the rack (Cake will continue to set as it cools).

12. Refrigerate cake, loosely covered for at least 6 hours. Remove side of pan, transfer cake to a plate and bring to room temperature before serving.

LEVEL OF DIFFICULTY ★★★

Red Velvet Weed Cake

120 minutes PREP TIME

★ ★ ★

» This is a very delicious Ganja laced red velvet chocolate cake that will leave your tasetbuds begging for more!

🛒 SHOPPING LIST

- 2- 9-inch cake pans
- cooking spray
- 2 cups all-purpose flour
- 2 tablespoons cocoa powder
- 1½ teaspoons baking soda

- 1 teaspoon salt
- ½ cup CannaButter, softened
- 1½ cups sugar
- 1 teaspoon vanilla extract
- 1 tablespoon red food coloring

- 2 eggs
- 4 tablespoons all-purpose flour
- 1 cup milk
- 1 cup sugar
- 1 cup butter, softened (or CannaButter)

🍲 DIRECTIONS

1. Preheat oven to 350 degrees. Grease both 9-inch cake pans with cooking spray.

2. Mix together flour, cocoa powder, baking soda and salt. Set aside.

3. Beat together CannaButter, sugar and vanilla in a separate bowl. Add eggs and red food coloring. Mix well.

4. Add the flour mixture and buttermilk gradually to the CannaButter mixture. Beat well until everthing is well blended.

5. Pour batter into prepared pans.

6. Bake for 30 minutes in preheated oven, or until toothpick comes out clean. Cool for 10 minutes.

7. Remove cakes from the pan and allow to cool completely on wire racks.

8. Make icing by heating 4 tablespoons of flour and 1 cup of milk in a saucepan over low heat. Stir constantly until mixture thickens. Let cool completely.

9. Beat in 1 cup of sugar and 1 cup of butter to the Flour/Milk mix. Beat until frosting reaches desired consistency.

10. Wait for cake layers to cool before frosting.

11. Spread a layer of icing on the top of one layer of cake. Set the dry layer ontop of the iced layer to make a sandwich.

12. Use the remaining icing to frost the entire cake and then Store in the refrigerator.

Bud Crispy Treats

15 minutes PREP TIME

>> Hands down the easiest weed edible dessert you'll make. Quick to create and easy to get addicted.

🛒 SHOPPING LIST

- 1/2 cup of marijuana butter
- 4 cups miniature marshmallows
- 5 cups of Rice Crispy treats cereal or any crisp rice cereal

LEVEL OF DIFFICULTY ★★★

🍲 DIRECTIONS

1. Melt margarine in large sauce pan over low heat. Add marshmallows and stir until melted and well-blended.

2. Cook 2 minutes longer, stirring constantly. Remove from heat and add cereal. Stir until well coated.

3. Using buttered spatula or waxed paper, press mixture evenly and firmly in buttered 13 x 9 inch pan. Cut into 2 x 2 inch squares when cool.

4. Eat! Remember to start with a 1/4 or 1/2 of the treat to make sure you don't intake too much at once. Some edibles take 1-2 hours to kick in fully.

Peace, Love & Happiness. Have a Blessed Day!
Please visit our website and check out the
rest of Uprock Publications books

www.uprockpublications.com

9780692518656